DOS
Disk Analyzer

Ronald A. Thisted

Produced by:
Brian Wiser & Bill Martens

 Apple PugetSound Program Library Exchange

DOS Disk Analyzer

www.callapple.org

ISBN: 978-0-359-74827-3

ACKNOWLEDGEMENTS

DOS Disk Analyzer was programmed by Ronald A. Thisted and published by A.P.P.L.E. in 1983, and is © copyright 1983 Ronald A. Thisted.

PRODUCTION

Brian Wiser → Cover, Design, Layout, Editing
Bill Martens → Scanning, Initial Manual, Software Updates

DISCLAIMER

About Ronald A. Thisted

Ronald A. Thisted was an early member of the Apple Pugetsound Program Library Exchange and an avid reader of Call-A.P.P.L.E. magazine. He has been a professor at the University of Chicago and is the current Vice Provost.

A graduate of both Pomona College and Stanford University, Ronald's specialty is mathematics and statistics.

About the Producers

Brian Wiser

Brian Wiser is a producer of books, films, games, and events, as well as a long-time consultant, enthusiast and historian of Apple, the Apple II and Macintosh. Steve Wozniak and Steve Jobs, as well as *Creative Computing*, *Nibble*, *InCider*, and *A+* magazines were early influences.

Brian designed, edited, and co-produced dozens of books including: *Nibble Viewpoints: Business Insights From The Computing Revolution*, *Cyber Jack: The Adventures of Robert Clardy and Synergistic Software*, *Synergistic Software: The Early Games*, *The Colossal Computer Cartoon Book: Enhanced Edition*, *All About Applesoft: Enhanced Edition*, *Graphically Speaking: Enhanced Edition*, *What's Where in the Apple: Enhanced Edition*, and *The WOZPAK: Special Edition* – an important Apple II historical book with Steve Wozniak's restored original, technical handwritten notes. Brian is also the author of *The Etch-a-Sketch and Other Fun Programs*.

He passionately preserves and archives all facets of Apple's history, and noteworthy companies such as Beagle Bros and Applied Engineering, featured on AppleArchives.com. His writing, interviews and books are featured on the technology news site CallApple.org and in *Call-A.P.P.L.E.* magazine that he co-produces as an A.P.P.L.E. board member. Brian also co-produced the retro iOS game *Structris*.

In 2005, Brian was cast as an extra in Joss Whedon's movie *Serenity*, leading him to being a producer and director for the documentary film *Done The Impossible: The Fans' Tale of Firefly & Serenity*. He brought some of the *Firefly* cast aboard his Browncoat Cruise and recruited several of the *Firefly* cast to appear in a film for charity. Throughout these experiences, he develops close personal relationships with many actors, authors, and computer industry luminaries. Brian speaks about his adventures to large audiences at conventions around the country.

Bill Martens

Bill Martens is a systems engineer specializing in office infrastructures and has been programming since 1976. The DEC PDP 11/40 with ASR-33 Teletypes and CRT's were his first computing platforms with his first forays in the Apple world coming with the Apple II computer.

Influences in Bill's computing life came from *Byte* magazine, *Creative Computing* magazine, and *Call-A.P.P.L.E.* magazine as well as his mentors Samuel Perkins, Don Williams, Joff Morgan, and Mike Christensen.

Bill is the author of *ApPilot/W1*, *Beyond Quest*, *The Anatomy of an EAMON*, and multiple EAMon adventure games, as well as a co-producer of many books including *What's Where in the Apple: Enhanced Edition*, *The WOZPAK: Special Edition*, *Nibble Viewpoints: Business Insights From The Computing Revolution*, and co-programmer for the iOS version of the retro game *Structris*. He has written many articles which have appeared in user group newsletters and magazines such as *Call-A.P.P.L.E.*.

Bill worked for Apple Pugetsound Program Library Exchange (A.P.P.L.E.) under Val Golding and Dick Hubert as a data manager and programmer in the 1980s, and is the current president of the A.P.P.L.E. user group established in 1978. He reorganized A.P.P.L.E. and restarted *Call-A.P.P.L.E.* magazine in 2002. He is the production editor for the A.P.P.L.E. website CallApple.org, writes science fiction novels in his spare time, and is a retired semi-pro football player.

CONTENTS

* Introduction *

The idea for a DOS disk analysis program (and ultimately, for this article) began when I received a copy of the first few disks in the *Eamon Adventure* series through A.P.P.L.E.'s "as is" software bank. After playing through the *Beginner's Cave*, I decided I wanted to learn more about the structure of the Adventure programs, so I loaded the *Eamon* #0 disk and ran the program to print manuals. About a third of the way into the dungeon master's manual – just as things were beginning to get interesting – my printer spewed out some garbage and stopped.

The *Eamon* system prints the manuals using a short Applesoft program which reads the text of the manual from a TEXT file and sends it to the printer. A quick look at the disk catalog indicated that the manual occupied 123 sectors on the disk. A quick estimate of the number of lines printed before disaster struck was about 250 forty-column lines. Quickly recalling that DOS sectors hold 256 bytes each (or about six 40-column lines), I figured that only about 40 sectors worth of manual had made it as far as my printer. I asked myself, "Where is the rest of the manual?" My quickness deserted me, and it was time for a slower, more methodical approach.

Although I suspected that the problem was on the disk, the first order of business was to rule out a problem with either the printer itself or the program printing the text file. The printer was easily eliminated as the source of the problem by LISTing a program and by printing the dungeon user's manual. Rather than test the supplied printing program itself, however, I used a program of my own which lists text files. It collapsed at the same point – and in the same way – as the one supplied on the *Eamon* disk.

At this point, had I purchased the software from a dealer, I would have gone back and asked for replacement or refund. But the *Eamon* disks are sold "as is," after all, and the disk itself was *physically* okay, so that meant that I was on my own. The first question that I wanted to answer was whether or not the rest of the manual actually was still somewhere on the disk. If so, I wanted to know where it was, and also, I wanted to print it out. That meant that I would have to do some exploration in a domain every bit as challenging as most Adventures.

There are some excellent tools available for doing disk exploration. Two of these tools are the A.P.P.L.E. *Diskpak 6B-16*, with its DISK ZAP program, and *Beneath Apple DOS* by Don Worth and Pieter Lechner. DISK ZAP is a program that allows you to look at individual sectors on a DOS 3.3 disk, to edit and modify the contents of the sector, and even (shudder!) to write these changes back onto the disk. This kind of exploration is not for amateur adventurers. *Beneath Apple DOS* tells you everything you could ever want to know about DOS 3.3, including the formats for the disks, how data is organized on the disk, and where everything is on the standard DOS 3.3 disk. In addition, Worth and Lechner tell you the formats used for different kinds of files. A third tool, which will be sufficient for this article, is *The DOS Manual* supplied with DOS 3.3.

Suppose we wished to print a text file called "DOCUMENT" which is 123 pages long. Let's see how DOS goes about it. First of all, we have to know that all files are stored in chunks called *sectors*, and these sectors are stored in concentric rings on the disk called *tracks*. There are 35 tracks on each standard diskette, and each contains 16 sectors. To find a particular sector, we must supply a track number (between 0 and 34) and a sector number (between 0 and 15). Together, these give the *track/sector address* of the particular sector we are interested in. Now to get at DOCUMENT, we have to look up that name in the disk catalog.

But even before that, we have to find out where the catalog itself is on the disk. That information is contained in the sector called the Volume Table of Contents (VTOC), and on a standard disk the VTOC is always on track 17, sector 0 – the track right in the middle of the diskette. The VTOC contains quite a bit of housekeeping information, including the track/sector address of the catalog. The catalog can be quite long and often occupies far more than a single sector. Each sector, in fact, will hold only seven catalog entries. Consequently, the VTOC actually contains the address of only the *first* catalog sector.

That first catalog sector contains the first seven catalog entries, and it also contains the track/sector address of the second catalog sector (which contains the next seven entries). The second catalog sector contains the address of the third, and so on, making it possible to have catalogs that are arbitrarily long. This way of organizing the catalog is called a *singly-linked list*; from each link in the chain, you can determine the next link. (In a *doubly-linked list*, each item would contain the address of the item before it in the chain, as well as the address of the one following it. Such data structures are often used, but for the disk catalog would be of little value.)

Using the VTOC, we can go to the first sector of the catalog and see DOCUMENT has an entry there. If not, we can go to the next catalog sector, and so on, until we find the catalog entry for the file name we are seeking. The catalog entry contains information about the file itself, including its length, whether it is locked, and the disk address of the file's *track/sector list*, which will finally tell us where the sectors of the file itself are.

Just as the catalog could be a chain many sectors long, the file itself is usually many sectors long. The catalog is chained using a linked list, and the VTOC points to the first link in the chain. The information for the file, on the other hand, is stored in a table containing the addresses of the various sectors in the file. This list is called the track/sector list. Each sector of the track/sector list can hold up to 122 entries. By going to the sectors indicated by this table in order, we can extract the file itself. [There is one further complication. If the file is longer than 122 sectors, a single track/sector list sector is not enough! In this case, the several track/sector list sectors are themselves connected by another singly-linked list.]

As a review, to get to the 83rd sector of a text file called "DOCUMENT", we must first read the VTOC to find the catalog, then search the catalog to find the track/sector list for DOCUMENT, then we must find element number 83 in the track/sector list, and then go to *that* track and sector address to read the desired portion of DOCUMENT. It is almost like finding your way through a maze of twisty little passages, all different.

To search through things in this fashion is fairly easy using DISK ZAP, in that all you need to do is to supply a track/sector combination and ZAP will retrieve the specified sector from the disk. Unfortunately, to review this information, you have to be a wizard at decoding hexadecimal numbers, and you also have to be pretty good at

3

counting bytes so that you are certain that you are decoding the right bytes at the right time. Of course, you also have to have a copy of *Beneath Apple DOS* next to you as your map to the maze.

A second problem is that, once you get to the sectors of interest, it is nearly impossible to determine whether they contain a portion of the manual that you have seen or not, since to do that requires laborious translation of the hexadecimal notation to the (readable) ASCII character equivalent. [DISK ZAP would tell you, for instance, that this paragraph, up through the second word, is A0 A0 A0 A0 C1 A0 F3 E5 E3 EF EE E4 (if I did the translation right)]. A half hour of this can easily lead to frustration, boredom, loss of interest, or all of the above. But the kinds of things that make the task so demanding and frustrating are also the kinds of things that Apples are good at doing.

So why not write a program that will do all of this chaining and translating for us? That thought led me to the *Disk Analyzer* program which is described below. It is an interesting program to study, educational to use, and illustrates (I hope) several aspects of good programming practice.

Designing the Program

The purpose of the program is to read specified sectors from the disk, to decode each, and to present the information in a form readable by the user of the program. There are four different types of sectors: VTOC, catalog, track/sector list, and text.

The information in each kind of sector is stored in a different way, so the program will have to be able to decode and display information in each of these formats. This describes what the program must do, at a minimum, to solve the problem. But before writing the program itself, it is important to think about what else the program should do.

For instance, it should be able to read a diskette in either drive, so an option to select the appropriate drive must be included. It would be useful to have a printed copy of the results at any point, so some provision must be made for sending results to the printer. It would also be nice to let the user of the program choose where the output will go (and when).

The outline of a program is starting to take shape. Each time the user is asked for input, he or she should be able to:

1. Read a sector from the disk and interpret it according to one of the four formats,

2. Turn the printer on or off,

3. Determine the disk drive from which the next sector will be read, or

4. Quit the program. If a sector is to be read, then the user must also supply the disk address, that is, the track and sector numbers, of the sector in question. We should also make certain that the disk addresses provided are valid ones -- track between 0 and 34, sector between 0 and 15. We can outline all of this as follows:

```
repeat

    get command from user

    if command=P then turn printer off/on

    if command=D then switch to other disk drive

    if command=Q then we are DONE

    if command asks to display a sector then

      repeat

        get track and sector

      until track and sector are both valid

      read the appropriate sector

      interpret and display using specified format

    if command=anything else then tell the user it's not valid
until we are DONE.
```

In a sense, we have solved the problem. Everything from here on in is simply elaboration and refinement of the outline given above. Some parts of the outline, such as getting a command from the user, are very easy to translate into Applesoft. Indeed, the statement:

```
        INPUT "COMMAND: ";C$
```

is just about all it takes. Other parts of the program will require much more elaboration; there is a lot of programming implied by the phrase "interpret and display" in the outline. However, we can take this subproblem, make an outline for it, and deal with it one part at a time. This method is called *top-down programming*, and is a good way to write programs in general.

Top-down or *structured* programming usually produces programs which consist of small "chunks", each of which can be understood by itself. Each chunk performs a single specific task, and can be thought of as a building block from which the program is made. Programs written in this way are often easier to understand and easier to debug. A pleasant by-product is that it is also relatively easy to add new chunks to do new things without interfering in the correct operation of the existing parts of the program. The *Disk Analyzer* program was developed in this way. Although it would be interesting to go through the stages which led to the ultimate program presented here, it would take us too far afield to do so. Nevertheless, its building-block structure should be apparent.

* RWTS: Reading the Disk *

The tool we shall use to do the actual reading from the disk is the same one that DOS uses to read a sector, a subroutine called RWTS (for "Read or Write a Track and Sector"). The details of this subroutine are described in *The DOS Manual* on pages 94-98. An assembly language version of a subroutine which sets up the call to RWTS to read a given sector from the disk is given in Listing 1.

This program will reside on the disk as a binary file which the *Disk Analyzer* program will BLOAD at the start of the program. Most of this program is not really a program at all, but rather a table of information that DOS needs to accomplish the reading task. The main table is called the IOB (for "Input/Output control Block") and contains the slot and drive numbers, the track and sector numbers, a code which indicates whether we desire to read, write, or (gulp!) initialize the diskette, and space for DOS to return an error code if something goes wrong. We also must provide DOS with 256 bytes of memory in which to place a copy of the sector being read (or from which to write the sector, if that is what we are doing). The address of this 256 byte *buffer* is also put in the IOB. There is a small program at the top which tells DOS where to find the IOB, and which then calls the RWTS subroutine itself. The details of the assembly language routine can be skipped; it is quite possible to go from here directly to the next section.

The subroutine in Listing 1 is called RWTSSUB, for obvious reasons. It is fairly easy to understand by stepping through it a line at a time. Incidentally, the listing was prepared using *BIG MAC.LC*, an A.P.P.L.E. assembler. The line numbers (starting with 1) are on the left-middle of the listing. To the *left* of the line numbers are the addresses and assembled code. To the *right* of the line numbers are the assembly language instructions. Assembly instructions have three parts, a label, the instruction (called the "opcode"), and the operand. It is good practice to describe the program by putting additional comments on each line; everything following a semicolon is considered a comment. Lines which begin with an asterisk are also considered to consist entirely of comments.

9

The first line is a comment containing the date and time at which the program was assembled. Since assembly language programs often go through a great many revisions before they are just right, it is helpful to have such a comment line in the program to identify just which version is most recent. This is helpful in writing programs in other languages as well, although I don't usually put the time of day in BASIC or Pascal programs.

Lines 3-9 contain basic descriptive information about what the program does, and information necessary to use it. Here we remind ourselves that this program will reside in page 3 of Apple memory, calls RWTS, contains its own IOB, and uses a buffer located at address $4000, inside the Hi-Res page 2 screen.

Lines 11 and 12 define two quantities for the assembler. BUFFER contains the address at which the 256 byte sector will be stored when it is read from the disk, and RWTSADDR contains the address at which the RWTS subroutine can be called. If either of these ever changed, for instance, if the Hi-Res screen were needed, then all we would have to do would be to change the address *here*, and it would be automatically changed wherever needed in the rest of the program. This is much better than putting in the actual address wherever needed, since to modify the program would then require sifting through to find every occurrence of the particular address.

The program itself starts in line 14. At line 14 is a command to the assembler to put the generated program at address $300, that is, at the start of page 3. Line 15 tells the assembler the name of the subroutine and its address (the "*" means "right here" to the assembler). The next two lines load accumulator and the Y register with the two halves of the IOB address, since the RWTS subroutine expects the IOB address to be stored in this fashion. Line 18 jump sent lines which immediately precede them. If the carry bit is set, then that means an error of some sort occurred while reading the disk. In this case, IBSTAT contains a code indicating what sort of error was detected. The BCC instruction Branches if the Carry bit is Clear; so if it is *set*, we simply continue on to the next instruction (line 29) which returns to the program that initially called this subroutine.

If the carry bit is clear (that is, not set) then the program branches to CLRERR, at line 30. This short routine loads the accumulator with zero, stores this value in IBSTAT, and then returns to the calling program. This is necessary, since if no error occurs, the content of IBSTAT is unpredictable. This way, if no error occurs, IBSTAT will always be zero when the program returns. The *Disk Analyzer* program will print the error code if IBSTAT returns anything other than zero. The codes are given on page 97 of *The DOS Manual*. Incidentally, I have used the same names for the IOB and DCTB variables that are described in *The DOS Manual*, so if you want to read more about them, you can refer directly to that manual.

The rest of the program defines the IOB table and an auxiliary table describing the disk drive called the Device Characteristics Table. The IOB contains initial values which may be changed by the *Disk Analyzer* program. IBSLOT contains the slot number of the disk to be read, multiplied by 16; IBDRVN contains the drive number of the disk to be read. In order to change from one drive to the other, the *Disk Analyzer* program will merely have to poke a different value into IBDRVN. Similarly, IBTRK and IBSECT give the track and sector to be read, and the *Disk Analyzer* program will poke values here after it gets them from the user. IBBUFP is a two-byte address of the buffer into which the 256 bytes of the sector will be read. This address is PEEKed at by *Disk Analyzer*. The current version puts the buffer into Hi-Res Page 2.

The most critical byte in the IOB is IBCMD. This byte determines which RWTS function will be carried out. A code of 1 will *read* a sector into the buffer. A code of 2 will *write* the contents of the buffer onto the sector. Before doing this, we had best be certain that the contents of the buffer are exactly what we want on the disk, because if we make a mistake there is no way to recover. An even more dangerous code is 4, which initializes the entire disk, wiping out everything that may have been on it. That is why it is always a good idea to make a backup diskette, and to use the backup rather than the original for testing purposes. When you type in the *Disk Analyzer* program, I heartily suggest that you use a backup diskette until you are certain that the program is working properly, even though the program is only supposed to read the disk. It is all too easy to mistype something and end up with disaster.

The remainder of the IOB contains additional information for RWTS, together with IBSTAT, the error return code discussed above.

* Disk Analyzer *

The *Disk Analyzer* is written in Applesoft, and is divided into several sections. Before giving a detailed description of the program and how it works, we shall first take an overview of the program (see Listing 2). Line numbers from 0 to 99 are reserved for identifying information. Lines 100 to 499 are used for setting up the program, and are executed only once, when the program is first run. Lines 500 to 999 contain the main body of the program. The code contained here is executed repeatedly. Lines 10000 to the end are reserved for "cleaning house" before stopping the program. All of the rest of the program (lines 1000 to 9999) contain subprograms used in the main routine. Note that the first three sections (identification, setup, and main loop) are each very short. As a result, each is easily understood. This is quite an advantage should we ever decide to add a new capability or to modify an old one.

The sections of code beginning at lines 1000, 2000, 3000, and 4000, respectively display the contents of a sector in each of four formats – VTOC, Catalog, Track/Sector List, and Text. The lines beginning at 8000 contain several very short utility programs, which do such things as turn the printer on (or off), print error messages, and clear the screen. The routine starting at 9000 sets up and calls the RWTSSUB program described above. Note that each of these pieces is also very short – none takes more than a page of listing. By breaking up large tasks into smaller, more easily understood tasks, it is possible to write programs that are easier to understand, easier to debug, and easier to modify. More importantly, they are also more likely to work correctly. With this overview, we can now proceed to look at the program in detail.

Starting at the beginning, lines 10 to 60 identify the author and the name of the program. Lines 40 and 50 contain two Applesoft statements which set the version number of the program, and the date on which it was completed. These values will be displayed whenever the program is run. I also use the version number in the name of the disk file, this helps me keep track of which version of the program is most recent.

13

Version 1.3 is, I confess, not the first version of this program. It is the third. This version is much more readable, much easier to use, and produces nicer output than the first version of the program. It is almost always the case that after writing and using a program, we have a much better idea how it *should* have been written and what it *ought* to do. In this case, I took the trouble to fix a lot of things that I didn't like about the first version. It is not terribly interesting work, but when other people are likely to use the program, it is worth the effort.

Lines 100-299 set things up for the main program. We make certain that we are in TEXT mode, clear the screen, point to disk drive 1 as the drive from which we will be reading, and set a variable that turns the printer off. Line 180 loads the RWTSSUB subroutine from the disk. (Instructions for how to get it there in the first place are given later.)

In line 190 we set the address of RWTSSUB to 768 (=$300). Should this ever change, it would only be necessary to modify this single statement to point to the new address, since the IOB address and the buffer address are determined from the address of RWTSSUB. The variable BASE extracts the buffer address from the IOB (line 210), and the function FNA(T) is defined to extract the T-th byte from the start of the buffer. Lines 230 to 250 define three strings that contain:

1. The valid commands which require a disk address

2. The valid commands which do not require a disk address

3. The complete collection of valid commands.

These are stored, respectively, in the strings VD$, VO$, and V$. The position of the commands in VD$ is important, since the first command will cause the program to go to the subroutine at line 1000, the second command in V$ will go to 2000, and so forth. Finally, in line 260 the user is given the opportunity to provide a line of identification for the disk being studied. This line will be printed whenever printed output is requested by the user.

The main loop starts at line 500. First of all, the printer is turned off and the headings for the screen are displayed, using subroutines for that purpose. (By removing the details of turning off the printer from the main program, we have made the main program itself much easier to follow. That's part of structured programming.)

At line 530 we ask the user to supply a command. In doing so, we provide the user with a complete list of all of the valid commands. If we wanted to be even more friendly to the user, we could display a menu describing the valid commands. To do this, we would simply add line 525 GOSUB 8900, and at 8900 we would write a program to display a suitable menu. After getting the command in the string C$, we set an error flag to zero and then we check to see if the command is a valid one. The subroutine which does the checking also does two other things. If the command is valid, but requires a disk address in order to complete, it sets the variable DISK to 1. In this case it also sets the variable JADR to the command number, determined by the position of the command in the string VD$. Second, the routine sets the variable VLD to 0 if the command is invalid, otherwise, VLD will be greater than zero.

At line 560, if the command is not valid, we print a message and then go back to the top of the loop. If no disk address information is required, we go to line 620 and skip the additional prompts required to obtain it. If we do have a DISK command, then the user must supply the track and sector to read, and we must check that these values are legitimate. This done, we can handle the commands. Line 670 turns the printer off it was on, and vice versa. Line 680 switches from disk 1 to 2, and vice versa. In each case, we go back to the top of the loop after setting the appropriate variable. If the user wishes to quit, line 690 directs control to the cleanup program at the very end (line 10000). Line 700 is a bit tricky. The N command gets the Next sector, if that makes sense. It will make sense whenever the current sector points to the next item in a singly-linked list. The variable NT always contains the address of the Next Track, and NS the address of the Next Sector. The variables T and S are used to determine which track and sector to read from the disk, so they are set to NT and NS at line 700. Sometimes there is no logical "next sector" which the program can determine. In this case, the variable JADR will have previously been set to zero. If this occurs, then a message is given to the user, and the program goes back to the top of the main loop.

15

Once all of this is taken care of, the program actually reads the desire sector from the disk at line 710. If an error occurred, a message is printed. Otherwise, the printer is activated if printing is on, and the appropriate subroutine is called at line 730. When the program returns from this subroutine, we continue back to the top of the main loop.

The "V" command interprets a sector as a Volume Table of Contents, and this is done in lines 1000-1180. First of all, we display the screen header, and then we notify the user that this is VTOC information. Lines 1030 to 1060 extract the information from the image of the sector stored in the buffer. The format for the VTOC is given on pages 132-133 of *The DOS Manual*. Thus, bytes 1 and 2 give the track and sector of the first catalog sector. In line 1030, for instance, NT=FNA(1) peeks at the first byte paste beginning of the buffer, and stores this result in NT, which then contains the track on which from the VTOC in a similar pattern uses lines 1070 to 1150 display them in a sensible fashion. Line 1160 goes to a subroutine which waits for the user to give the signal to continue. Since the most logical choice for the "next sector" to look at is the first directory sector, JADR is set to 2 before returning. That way, if the next command is the N command, the next sector (at track/sector = NT/NS) will automatically be interpreted using the correct format.

Lines 2000-2440 display a Catalog sector in response to the "C" command. The format for these sectors is given in *The DOS Manual* on pages 129-131. As before, we first display screen header information, then we extract the track/sector address of the next Catalog sector, if any, in NT/NS. (If there is none, these will be 0/0.) Each catalog sector can hold seven entries, which we loop through starting at line 2060. The array A$ will hold the name of the file, and FPTR will point to the start of the current entry. Each entry is 35 bytes long, and the first one follows 11 bytes of other information, which accounts for the cryptic formula for FPTR in 2070. The variables TP and SP point to the first track/sector list for the file, and TYPE identifies the kind of file stored. Lines 2110 through 2130 extract the name of the file from the buffer and put it into A$, which is then printed, and the length of the file in sectors is also computed. To delete a file, DOS replaces TP with the value 255 (hexadecimal $FF) in the catalog to act as a signal, and the Track of the track/sector list is stored in the last byte of the file name. We print "[D]" as an indicator that a file has been deleted. Following each file name, we print a notation giving where the track/sector list is located (first extracting the track number from its hiding place if the file had been deleted). The two lines at 2200 and 2205 are a device to make certain that exactly two spaces are used for track and sector printing, since Applesoft prints the smallest number of digits necessary when displaying numbers. The subroutine at 8800 does this task. This insures that the columns will be aligned appropriately on the output of this program.

Lines 2210-2330 determine if the file is locked, and lines 2240-2310 decode the file type. The last item printed for each file is the length of the file in sectors. When each file entry has been processed, we wait for the user to type a character, and then we go on to line 2430. The logical "next sector" to look at is the next directory sector. Since NT and NS point to the next sector, and since JADR already equals 2 (for directory format), there is no need to change anything to set things up for the "N" command – unless NT and NS are both zero, that is! In that case, there is no next catalog sector, and we set JADR to zero, so that the "N" command will be able to recognize this fact and act accordingly.

To look at a file, we must first find it, and that is what the track/sector list enables us (and DOS) to do. In response to the "T" command, lines 3000-3200 display a sector in track/sector format, which is described on pages 128-129 of *The DOS Manual*. Each sector holds up to 122 track/sector pairs. As usual we set up the screen and obtain the address of the next track/sector List sector. Since most files ordinarily are less than 122 sectors long, this will usually be 0/0, to indicate that no continuation is necessary. If this *is* a continuation list, however, the number of sectors described on previous lists is recorded in the sector offset bytes; we compute this quantity in line 3040. At line 3110 we start to loop through all 122 items in the list. Once again, we use the formatting subroutine at 8800 to make our columns look nice; otherwise they would weave in and out. Every time we print a track/sector pair we keep a count, and after every sixth one, we start a new line (lines 3150-3160). When we are all done, we again wait for the user to respond, and once again we check to see if there is a logical "next sector". Ordinarily there will not be, but if this is one of several track/sector lists for a very long file, then NT and NS will point to the next part of the list, and, of course, JADR will already be 3.

The final display routine prints an ASCII version of the sector. The command to do this is "X". Here, the screen and the printer are treated somewhat differently, since control characters can make some printers (including mine) go crazy. At lines 4010 and 4020 we display identifying information which depends on whether the printer is selected or not. We then break the sector into four 64-byte chunks, which we deal with one at a time. Each time through we build a 64-byte long string A$ which we print to the screen or the printer. In line 4060 we strip off the top bit from each byte (some printers require this). Then in line 4070, if we are printing the results, we replace each control character (those with ASCII codes less than 32) by a period (ASCII 46). Then in either case, we add the new character to the end of A$. When this chunk has been built, we print it and go on to the next chunk. As before, we allow the user to tell the program when to continue, and, since there is no logical "next sector", we set JADR to zero before returning to the main loop.

Most of the utility routines which start at line 8000 are straightforward to understand and do common things, so I shall not spend much time describing them. Routine 8000 clears the screen, prints the current track and sector, and prints the identifying line. Routine 8200 activates the printer. Any initialization and switching on that must be done should be done right here; what needs to be done will depend on the printer you have and which slot it is in.

I have a C. Itoh Prowriter printer attached to a Micro-buffer II interface in Slot 1, which this code is designed for. Routine 8300 turns off the printer, and here, too, you may have to write your own program to do this. Routine 8400 displays a message at the bottom of the screen and waits for the user to type any key in response. Of interest here is line 8445. While waiting for the user to reply, the program issues X=FRE(0). This instruction initiates garbage collection of the Applesoft string area. This is necessary because both commands "C" and "T" make extensive use of strings. Without this command, Applesoft's strings soon overwrite the Hi-Res graphics page – which is where the data we are operating on lives! This way, garbage collection is done regularly, and at a time when the user is looking at the output. As a consequence, I have never noticed a garbage-collection delay while using this program.

Routine 8500 checks the command entered by the user for validity, and sets up the variables JADR, VLD, and DISK. Routine 8600 prints the "Invalid Command" error message, and routine 8700 prints the "No next sector" message. Routine 8800 formats an integer to occupy exactly L% spaces when printed, by building a string exactly L% characters long.

The routine at 9000 pokes the track, sector, and drive to be read into the appropriate places in the IOB of RWTSSUB, and then RWTSSUB is called. Before returning, the subroutine checks to see if there were any disk errors, and if so, a message is printed. The code at 10000 is merely anything needed to clean things up before leaving. In my case, I make certain that the left margin of the printer is reset to zero if I have been using the printer. For other people, very little of this routine may be necessary. Still, it is aesthetically pleasing to exit from the program at the very END.

* Using the Program *

      Before the program can be used, one thing remains to be done. The machine language routine RWTSSUB needs to be stored on the disk. There are two ways to do this. First of all, the assembly language program can be typed in using an assembler such as *BIG MAC.LC*, assembled, and then the object code stored on the disk under the name RWTSSUB. Alternatively, one can enter the Monitor by typing CALL -151, entering the starting address followed by a colon (300:), and then entering the list of hexadecimal codes given in Listing 3. (If you do this, do *not* type in the addresses in the left hand column.) The items must be separated from one another by a space, and the RETURN key should not be pressed until all 37 items have been entered. Once this is done type 300.324 so that you can check whether you entered things correctly. If so, your list should be identical to the one in Listing 3. Finally, type CTRL-C to return to Applesoft, and then type "BSAVE RWTSSUB,A$300,L$25". This will store the program on the disk as desired.

      Once the preliminaries are taken care of, you need only run the program. The first thing you will be asked for is a disk identifier; just type in the name of the diskette. You will then be in the main loop, asked for a command.

      The commands are:

```
V = read a sector as VTOC
C = read a sector as Catalog
T = read a sector as Track/Sector List
X = read a sector and print teXt
N = read Next sector
P = turn Printer on or off
D = change Disk drive
Q = Quit the program
```

      So what did happen to the Adventure manuals, you ask? From Exhibit 1, we see that the VTOC is at track 17, sector 0, as usual, and that the first catalog sector is at 17/15. The very first catalog sector contains the file of interest, DDD MANUAL.TEXT, the fifth entry in Exhibit 2. We note that this file has 123 sectors, and the track/sector list for it starts at track 22, sector 15.

Exhibit 3 shows what the track/sector list looks like. This output is truly remarkable. The track/sector list contains only 86 entries! That still leaves over half of the manual unaccounted for, though, and when I examined the last sector in the track/sector list (11/1) it looked just fine – but it had not been printed out. By searching through the sectors (see Exhibit 4 for an example), I found that sector 8/1 had been printed out just fine, and that sector 8/0 (which contains garbage) is exactly where my manual had stopped printing. The sectors which precede and which follow 8/0 look fine. Closer inspection of 8/0 using DISK ZAP reveals that after the last words in 8/0 there is a byte containing 0, which DOS interprets as the end-of-file marker for TEXT files, which explains why the printing program stopped.

So now I have unequivocal evidence that my *Eamon* #0 disk had been clobbered, and I will have to sift through the rest of the diskette to find out if there is anything that goes between 8/1 and 9/15 in the manual, whether it is still on the disk, and also whether there really are an extra 36 sectors of manual (the difference between the catalog length and the actual number of entries in the track/sector list). Fortunately, the *Disk Analyzer* will make that job quite a bit easier.

Exhibit 1

```
DOS DISK ANALYZER   VER 1.3 [1/26/83]
PRINTER ON   CURRENT T=17 S=0 DRIVE=2
--- EAMON #0 DISKETTE ---
INTERPRETING THIS SECTOR AS VTOC

FIRST CATALOG SECTOR AT T=17 S=15
CREATED BY DOS 3.3 VOLUME=254
MAX T/S PAIRS PER T/S-LIST SECTOR=122
LAST TRACK WITH ALLOC SECTORS=29
DIRECTION OF TRACK ALLOCATION=+1
TRACKS PER DISKETTE: 35
SECTORS PER TRACK:   16
BYTES PER SECTOR:    256
```

Exhibit 2

```
DOS DISK ANALYZER   VER 1.3 [1/26/83]
PRINTER ON   CURRENT T=17 S=15 DRIVE=2
--- EAMON #0 DISKETTE ---
NEXT CATALOG SECTOR IS AT 17/14


HELLO
-----T/S AT: 18/15 UNLOCKED APP LEN=3


-----T/S AT: 19/15 UNLOCKED TXT LEN=1
BASE DUNGEON PROGRAM
-----T/S AT: 20/15 UNLOCKED APP LEN=52
BASE DUNGEON PROGRAM (OLD)
-----T/S AT: 21/15 UNLOCKED APP LEN=52
DDD MANUAL.TEXT
-----T/S AT: 22/15 UNLOCKED TXT LEN=123
DUNGEON CREATE MENU
-----T/S AT: 23/15 UNLOCKED APP LEN=4
DUNGEON EDIT
-----T/S AT: 24/15 UNLOCKED APP LEN=37
```

Exhibit 3

```
DOS DISK ANALYZER  VER 1.3 [1/26/83]
PRINTER ON  CURRENT T=22 S=15 DRIVE=2
--- EAMON #0 DISKETTE ---
NEXT T/S LIST AT 0/0 OFFSET=0
22/14 22/13 22/12 22/11 22/10 22/ 9
22/ 8 22/ 7 22/ 6 22/ 5 22/ 4 22/ 3
22/ 2 22/ 1 22/ 0 7/ 7 7/ 6 7/ 5
 7/ 4 7/ 3 7/ 2 7/ 1 7/ 0 8/15
 8/14 8/13 8/12 8/11 8/10 8/ 9
 8/ 8 8/ 7 8/ 6 8/ 5 8/ 4 8/ 3
 8/ 2 8/ 1 8/ 0 9/15 9/14 9/13
 9/12 9/11 9/10 9/ 9 9/ 8 9/ 7
 9/ 6 9/ 5 9/ 4 9/ 3 9/ 2 9/ 1
 9/ 0 10/15 10/14 10/13 10/12 10/11
10/10 10/ 9 10/ 8 10/ 7 10/ 6 10/ 5
10/ 4 10/ 3 10/ 2 10/ 1 10/ 0 11/15
11/14 11/13 11/12 11/11 11/10 11/ 9
11/ 8 11/ 7 11/ 6 11/ 5 11/ 4 11/ 3
11/ 2 11/ 1 0/ 0 0/ 0 0/ 0 0/ 0
 0/ 0 0/ 0 0/ 0 0/ 0 0/ 0 0/ 0
 0/ 0 0/ 0 0/ 0 0/ 0 0/ 0 0/ 0
 0/ 0 0/ 0 0/ 0 0/ 0 0/ 0 0/ 0
 0/ 0 0/ 0 0/ 0 0/ 0 0/ 0 0/ 0
 0/ 0 0/ 0 0/ 0 0/ 0 0/ 0 0/ 0
 0/ 0 0/ 0
```

Exhibit 4

```
--- EAMON #0 DISKETTE ---
TRACK=11 SECTOR=1

nd you'll.have to change a few things..  .  .
THE END.....................................................
...........................................................
...........................................................
.........

--- EAMON #0 DISKETTE ---
TRACK=8 SECTOR=1

e room numbers.that you can get to from that room in.each dir
ection.  A special code has.been developed--if you give a
room of.0, you can never move that direction..If you give posi
tive direction, there's.an open connection. Negative numbers.

--- EAMON #0 DISKETTE ---
TRACK=8 SECTOR=0

"YOU TAKE A CLOSER LOOK AT YOUR RESCUER. HE IS RATHER DIRTY
BUT HAS A NICE FACE."..LY WAY TO GO IS TO MY HUT EAST."......
...........................................................
...........................................................
.........
```

Exhibit 5 (Listing 1)

```
*/ 26 January 83  2:58 pm
  AST 25
*
* RWTSSUB
* Ronald A. Thisted
*
* This routine calls RWTS with an IOB in page 3. The sector-
* read buffer is located in Hi-Res page 2, at $4000
*
  AST 25
BUFFER EQU $4000 ;Address of sector read buffer
RWTSADDR EQU $3D9 ;Address of the RWTS subroutine
  AST 25
ORG $300 ;Load in page three
RWTSSUB EQU * ;RWTSSUB subroutine
  LDA #>IOB ;Load A and Y with a
  LDY #<IOB ; with address of IOB
  JSR RWTSADDR ;Go to the RWTS subroutine
*
* If the carry bit is set, then an error occured
* and IBSTAT contains the result. In this case
* we merely return to the caller with the error
* code intact. If the carry bit is NOT set, then
* IBSTAT contains garbage. In this case we set
* IBSTAT to zero as an indicator of an
* error-free condition.
*
  BCC CLRERR ;If carry clear, then clear IBSTAT
  RTS ;Else, return to sender with IBSTAT as is
CLRERR LDA #0 ;Load and
  STA IBSTAT ; store IBSTAT of zero
  RTS ;and then go back home.
*
* IOB FOLLOWS
*
IOB EQU *
IBTYPE DFB 1 ;IOB Type (must be 1)
IBSLOT DFB 6*16 ;Slot * 16
IBDRVN DFB 1 ;Drive number (initialized to 1)
IBVOL DFB 0 ;Volume number expected (0 matches any)
IBTRK DS 1 ;Track to read or write
IBSECT DS 1 ;Sector to read or write
IBDCTP DA DCTB ;Address of Device Characteristics Table
```

```
IBBUFP DA BUFFER ;Address of data buffer
IBDUMY DS 2 ;Unused
IBCMD DFB 1 ;1=Read (This program won't try anything else!)
IBSTAT DS 1 ;If carry set, then contains error code
IBSMOD DS 1 ;Volume number found will be stored here
IOBPSN DFB 6*16 ;Last Slot accessed (*16)
IOBPDN DFB 1 ;Last Drive accessed
*
* DCT FOLLOWS
*
DCTB EQU * ;Device Characteristics Table
DEVPTC DFB 0 ;Device type= DISK II (0)
PPTC DFB 1 ;Phases per track = 1
MONTC DFB $EF,$D8 ;Time count motor on (complemented)

New record at : 4508


Name      : READ
End of file  :  1,280
```

* A Few Notes on the Disk *

Originally, this program was written to accompany an article describing its development and use. The text of that article is contained in the two files DISK ANALYZE 1 and DISK ANALYZE 2. These are text files; an equivalent pair of binary files have the same name with a ".S" following.

The article refers to Exhibits 1 to 4, and these are contained in the text file EXHIBITS, which you should also print out. The article also refers to Listings 1 through 3. These listings are *not* contained on this disk. Listing 1 is the assembler listing of RWTSSUB. It can be obtained by running RWTSSUB through the BIG MAC.LC assembler. A somewhat less readable version is appended as Exhibit 5 to the EXHIBITS file. Listing 2 can be obtained by LOADing DISK ANALYZER 1.3 and then giving the LIST command. Listing 3 is a Monitor listing of RWTSSUB. To get a copy of Listing 3, BLOAD RWTSSUB, then enter the Monitor with CALL -151, then give the monitor command 300.325 – you can then leave the Monitor with a CTRL-C. The reason for not including these listings directly in the text is that it was very hard to redirect output from a printer to a disk file.

```
Name   : HELLO
Length : $0237 (567)
Load at : $0801 (2049)

  5 D$ = CHR$(4)
 10 TEXT
 20 HOME
 50 VTAB 8
 60 PRINT "ALL PROGRAMS ON THIS DISK WERE"
 70 PRINT "WRITTEN BY RONALD A. THISTED"
 80 VTAB 12
 90 PRINT "COPYRIGHT 1983 RONALD A. THISTED"
100 VTAB 15
110 PRINT "REPRODUCTION WITHOUT *WRITTEN*"
120 PRINT "PERMISSION IS PROHIBITED."
130 PRINT : PRINT
140 PRINT "1. LIST INSTRUCTIONS TO SCREEN"
145 PRINT "2. LIST INSTRUCTIONS TO PRINTER"
150 PRINT "3. RUN THE PROGRAM"
155 PRINT : PRINT "   WHICH? ";: GET Q$
157 PRINT
160 IF Q$ = "3" THEN PRINT D$;"RUN DISK ANALYZER 1.3"
165 IF Q$ = "2" THEN PRINT D$;"PR#1"
200 PRINT D$;"FILEDUMP READ"
210 PRINT D$;"FILEDUMP DOCS1"
220 PRINT D$;"FILEDUMP DOCS2"
230 PRINT D$;"FILEDUMP EXHIBITS"
240 PRINT D$;"PR#0
250 GOTO 130
```

```
Name   : DISK ANALYZER 1.3
Length : $1859 (6233)
Load at : $0801 (2049)

  10 REM --------------------------------
  20 REM - DOS DISK ANALYZER
  30 REM - RONALD A. THISTED
  40 VRS = 1.3: REM    VERSION NUMBER
  50 DT$ = "1/26/83": REM REVISION DATE
  60 REM ---------------------------------^J^J
 100 REM ------SETUP------
 110 TEXT
 120 HOME
 130 DR = 1: REM -SET DEFAULT DISK DRIVE
 140 P = 0: REM --SET DEFAULT PRINTER OFF
 150 BELL$ = CHR$(7): REM -BELL CHARACTER
 160 D$ = CHR$(4): REM ----DOS CHARACTER
 170 E$ = CHR$(27): REM ---ESC CHARACTER
 180 PRINT D$"BLOAD RWTSSUB"
 190 RWTSSUB = 768: REM  ADDRESS OF RWTS SUBROUTINE
 200 IOB = RWTSSUB + 16: REM ADDRESS OF IOB FOR RWTS
     SUBROUTINE
 210 BASE = PEEK(IOB + 8) + 256 * PEEK(IOB + 9): REM -
     ADDRESS OF SECTOR READ BUFFER
 220 DEF FNA(T) = PEEK(BASE + T)
 230 VD$ = "VCTX": REM VALID COMMANDS NEEDING DISK
     ADDRESS
 240 VO$ = "NPDQ": REM VALID COMMANDS NOT NEEDING DISK
     ADDRESS
 250 V$ = VD$ + VO$: REM ALL VALID COMMANDS
 260 PRINT "ENTER DISK IDENTIFICATION: ": INPUT ":";T$
 299 REM -----END OF SETUP-----^J^J
 500 REM -----MAIN LOOP-----
 510 GOSUB 8300: REM -DEACTIVATE PRINTER
 520 GOSUB 8000: REM -DISPLAY SCREEN HEADINGS
 530 PRINT "COMMAND ("V$;: INPUT "): ";C$
 540 ER = 0: REM -INITIALIZE ERROR FLAG TO 0
 550 GOSUB 8500: REM -SEE IF THIS COMMAND IS VALID
 560 IF NOT VLD THEN GOSUB 8600: GOTO 500: REM -INFORM
     USER AND REPROMPT
 570 IF NOT DISK THEN 620
```

```
580 INPUT "TRACK,SECTOR: ";T,S
590 IF (T < 0) OR (T > 34) THEN PRINT BELL$"INVALID
    TRACK NUMBER [0..34]": GOTO 580
600 IF (S < 0) OR (S > 15) THEN PRINT BELL$"INVALID
    SECTOR NUMBER [0..15]": GOTO 580
610 REM
620 REM -----------------------
630 REM -HANDLE REMAINING COMMANDS
640 REM -NOTE THAT DISK COMMANDS ARE ALREADY CODED IN
    JADR, WHICH
650 REM -WAS SET BY THE COMMAND CHECKER ROUTINE AT
    8500
660 REM -----------------------
670 IF C$ = "P" THEN P = 1 - P: GOTO 500: REM -TOGGLE
    PRINTER
680 IF C$ = "D" THEN DR = 3 - DR:GOTO 500: REM
    -TOGGLE DISK DRIVE
690 IF C$ = "Q" THEN GOTO 10000: REM -EXIT FROM
    PROGRAM
700 IF C$ = "N" THEN T = NT: S = NS: IF JADR = 0 THEN
    GOSUB 8700: GOTO 500: REM -NEXT SECTOR
710 IF DISK OR (C$ = "N") THEN GOSUB 9000: REM
    -SETUP AND CALL RWTSSUB TO GET SECTOR
715 IF ER < > 0 THEN GOSUB 8400: GOTO 500: REM
    -REPROMPT ON DISK ERROR
720 IF P = 1 THEN GOSUB 8200: REM -ACTIVATE PRINTER
730 ON JADR GOSUB 1000,2000,3000,4000
740 GOTO 500: REM -PROMPT AGAIN AFTER SUCCESSFUL
    COMPLETION OF CMD
750 REM -----END OF MAIN LOOP-----^J^J
1000 REM -VTOC FORMAT
1010 GOSUB 8000: REM -HEADER INFO
1020 PRINT "INTERPRETING THIS SECTOR AS VTOC": PRINT
1030 NT = FNA(1): NS = FNA(2): VER = FNA(3)
1040 VOL = FNA(6):MTS = FNA(39)
1050 LT = FNA(48): DIR = FNA(49)
1060 TPD = FNA(52): SPT = FNA(53): NB = FNA(54) +
       256 * FNA(55)
1070 PRINT "FIRST CATALOG SECTOR AT T="NT" S="NS
1080 PRINT "CREATED BY DOS 3."VER" VOLUME="VOL
1090 PRINT "MAX T/S PAIRS PER T/S-LIST SECTOR="MTS
```

```
1100 PRINT "LAST TRACK WITH ALLOC SECTORS="LT
1110 PRINT "DIRECTION OF TRACK ALLOCATION=";: IF DIR
     = 1 THEN PRINT "+1": GOTO 1130
1120 IF DIR = 255 THEN PRINT "-1": GOTO 1130
1125 PRINT DIR
1130 PRINT "TRACKS PER DISKETTE: ";TPD
1140 PRINT "SECTORS PER TRACK:  ";SPT
1150 PRINT "BYTES PER SECTOR:   ";NB
1160 GOSUB 8400
1170 JADR = 2
1180 RETURN: REM (FROM VTOC)^J^J
2000 REM ---CATALOG SECTORS---
2010 GOSUB 8000: REM -HEADER INFO
2030 NT = FNA(1): NS = FNA(2)
2040 PRINT "NEXT CATALOG SECTOR IS AT "NT"/"NS
2050 PRINT
2060 FOR I = 0 TO 6
2065  A$ = ""
2070  FPTR = 11 + I * 35
2080  TP = FNA(FPTR)
2090  SP = FNA(FPTR + 1)
2100  TYPE = FNA(FPTR + 2)
2110  FOR K = 3 TO 32
2120   A$ = A$ + CHR$( FNA(FPTR + K))
2130  NEXT K
2140  LNGTH = FNA(FPTR + 33) + 256 * FNA(FPTR + 34)
2150  PRINT A$;
2160  IF TP = 255 THEN PRINT "[D]";
2170  PRINT
2180  PRINT "-----T/S AT: ";
2190  IF TP = 255 THEN TP = FNA(FPTR + 32)
2200  L% = 2: X% = TP:GOSUB 8800: PRINT X$"/";
2205  X% = SP: GOSUB 8800: PRINT X$" ";
2210  IF TYPE < 128 THEN PRINT "UN";
2220  IF TYPE > 127 THEN PRINT " ";: TYPE = TYPE -
     128
2230  PRINT "LOCKED ";
2240  IF TYPE = 0 THEN PRINT "TXT ";: GOTO 2350
2250  IF TYPE = 1 THEN PRINT "INT ";: GOTO 2350
2260  IF TYPE = 2 THEN PRINT "APP ";: GOTO 2350
2270  IF TYPE = 4 THEN PRINT "BIN ";: GOTO 2350
```

```
2280  IF TYPE = 8 THEN PRINT "S   ";: GOTO 2350
2290  IF TYPE = 16 THEN PRINT "REL ";: GOTO 2350
2300  IF TYPE = 32 THEN PRINT "A   ";: GOTO 2350
2310  IF TYPE = 64 THEN PRINT "B   ";: GOTO 2350
2320  REM --UNKNOWN FILE TYPE
2330  PRINT "??? ";
2350  PRINT "LEN="LNGTH
2400 NEXT I
2410 PRINT : PRINT
2420 GOSUB 8400
2430 IF (NT = 0) AND (NS = 0) THEN JADR = 0
2440 RETURN: REM (FROM CATALOG)^J^J
3000 REM ---T/S LIST SECTORS---
3010 GOSUB 8000: REM -HEADER INFO
3020 NT = FNA(1)
3030 NS = FNA(2)
3040 SOFF = FNA(5) + 256 * FNA(6)
3050 PRINT "NEXT T/S LIST AT "NT"/"NS;
3060 PRINT " OFFSET="SOFF
3100 K = 0: REM -K COUNTS NUMBER OF T/S'S PRINTED ON
     LINE SO FAR
3110 FOR I = 12 TO 254 STEP 2
3120  L% = 2: X% = FNA(I): GOSUB 8800: A$ = X$
3130  L% = 2: X% = FNA(I + 1): GOSUB 8800: B$ = X$
3140   PRINT A$"/"B$" ";
3150   K = K + 1
3160   IF K = 6 THEN PRINT :  K = 0
3170 NEXT I
3180 GOSUB 8400
3190 IF (NT = 0) AND (NS = 0) THEN JADR = 0
3200 RETURN: REM (FROM T/S)^J^J
4000 REM ---TEXT DUMP---
4010 IF P = 0 THEN GOSUB 8000: GOTO 4030
4020 PRINT : PRINT T$: PRINT "TRACK="T" SECTOR="S:
     PRINT
4030 FOR I = 0 TO 255 STEP 64
4035  A$ = ""
4040  FOR J = 0 TO 63
4050   X = PEEK(BASE + I + J)
4060   IF X > 127 THEN X = X - 128
4070   IF (P = 1) AND (X < 32) THEN X = 46
```

```
4080   A$ = A$ + CHR$(X)
4090  NEXT J
4100   PRINT A$
4110 NEXT I
4120 GOSUB 8400
4130 JADR = 0
4140 RETURN: REM (FROM TEXT)^J^J
7900 REM -^J^JUTILITY ROUTINES^J^J
8000 REM -DISPLAY ROUTINE
8010 REM -PRINTER SHOULD BE DEACTIVATED FOR SCREEN
     DISPLAY
8020 VTAB 1
8030 PRINT "DOS DISK ANALYZER  VER "VRS" ["DT$"]";:
     CALL - 868: PRINT
8040 PRINT "PRINTER ";: IF P = 1 THEN INVERSE: PRINT
     "ON";:   NORMAL: PRINT "  ";: GOTO 8060
8050 PRINT "OFF ";
8060 PRINT "CURRENT T="T" S="S" DRIVE="DR;:  CALL -
     868:  PRINT
8070 CALL - 958: REM -CLEAR SCREEN
8080 PRINT T$
8090 VTAB 5
8100 RETURN:  REM (FROM HEADER DISPLAY)^J^J
8200 REM ---ACTIVATE PRINTER---
8210 PR#1
8220 REM ---C.ITOH/MB II SPECIFICS---
8230 PRINT E$"E"E$"L005
8240 RETURN:  REM (FROM PRINTER ACTIVATION)^J^J
8300 REM ---DEACTIVATE PRINTER---
8310 PR#0
8320 RETURN:  REM (FROM PRINTER DEACTIVATION)^J^J
8400 REM -PROMPT AND WAIT FOR KEYIN
8405 GOSUB 8300:  REM -DEACTIVATE PRINTER
8410 VTAB 24
8420 INVERSE
8430 PRINT "TYPE ANY KEY TO CONTINUE";:  NORMAL
8440 POKE - 16368,0:  REM CLEAR STROBE
8445 X = FRE(0):  REM -INITIATE GARBAGE COLLECTION
     OF STRINGS
8450 X = PEEK( - 16384):  IF X < 128 THEN 8450
8460 POKE - 16368,0
```

```
8470 PRINT
8480 RETURN:   REM (FROM ACKNOWLEDGEMENT ROUTINE)^J^J
8500 REM -CHECK TO SEE IF C$ IS KNOWN AND SET FLAGS
8510 VLD = 0:   REM -DEFAULT TO INVALID COMMAND
8520 DISK = 0:   REM - DEFAULT TO NOT-DISK COMMAND
8530 FOR I = 1 TO LEN(V$)
8540  IF C$ = MID$(V$,I,1) THEN VLD = I
8550 NEXT I
8560 IF VLD AND (VLD < = LEN(VD$)) THEN JADR = VLD:
     DISK = 1
8570 REM -AT THIS POINT VLD=COMMAND NUMBER (OR 0 IF
     NOT VALID)
8580 REM -AT THIS POINT DISK=1 IF AND ONLY IF A T/S
     ADDRESS IS NEEDED
8590 RETURN:   REM (FROM COMMAND ANALYZER)^J^J
8600 REM -INVALID COMMAND HANDLER
8610 VTAB 10
8620 INVERSE
8630 PRINT BELL$"INVALID COMMAND"
8640 NORMAL
8650 GOSUB 8400:   REM WAIT FOR ACKNOWLEDGEMENT
8660 RETURN:   REM (FROM INVALID CMD HANDLER)^J^J
8700 REM -NO NEXT SECTOR MESSAGE
8710 VTAB 10
8720 INVERSE
8730 PRINT BELL$"NO NEXT SECTOR IS DEFINED!"
8740 NORMAL
8750 GOSUB 8400:   REM -WAIT FOR ACKNOWLEDGEMENT
8760 RETURN:   REM (FROM NO NEXT SECTOR)^J^J^J^J^J^J^J
8800 REM -PRINT FORMATTED INTEGER
8810 REM -INPUT-L%=LENGTH
8820 REM -    -X%=VALUE
8830 REM OUTPUT-X$=STRING WITH FORMATTED VALUE
8840 X$ = STR$(X%)
8850 IF LEN(X$) > = L% THEN RETURN
8860 FOR Q = 1 TO L% - LEN(X$)
8870  X$ = " " + X$
8880 NEXT Q
8890 RETURN:   REM (FROM INTEGER FORMATTER)^J^J
```

```
8990 REM -^J^J^JRWTS CALLING SUBROUTINE^J^J
9000 REM --- RWTS STUFF ---
9010 POKE IOB + 4,T:  REM - SET TRACK
9020 POKE IOB + 5,S:  REM - SET SECTOR
9030 POKE IOB + 2,DR:  REM -SET DISK DRIVE
9040 CALL RWTSSUB
9050 REM --- ERROR CHECK---
9060 ER = PEEK(IOB + 13)
9070 IF ER < > 0 THEN PRINT BELL$"ERROR "ER"
     ENCOUNTERED!":  PRINT "RETURNING TO MAIN MENU."
9080 RETURN:   REM (FROM RWTS CALL)^J^J^J
9990 REM -^J^J^JCLOSING PROGRAM^J^J^J
10000 REM -CLEAN ENDINGS
10010 GOSUB 8300:   REM DEACTIVATE PRINTER
10020 VTAB 22
10030 REM ---CLEAN UP PRINTER
10040 REM ---C.ITOH SPECIFIC
10050 IF P = 0 THEN 10080
10060 PR#1
10070 PRINT E$"L000"
10080 PR#0
10090 END
```

```
Name   : RWTSSUB
Length : $0025 (37)
Load at : $0300


0300: A9 03        LDA #$03
0302: A0 10        LDY #$10
0304: 20 D9 03     JSR $03D9
0307: 90 01        BCC $030A
0309: 60           RTS
030A: A9 00        LDA #$00
030C: 8D 1D 03     STA $031D
030F: 60           RTS
0310: 01 60        ORA ($60,X)
0312: 01 00        ORA ($00,X)
0314: F7           ???
0315: E8           INX
0316: 21 03        AND ($03,X)
0318: 00           BRK
0319: 40           RTI
031A: F4           ???
031B: E8           INX
031C: 01 A0        ORA ($A0,X)
031E: D2 60        CMP ($60)
0320: 01 00        ORA ($00,X)
0322: 01 EF        ORA ($EF,X)
0324: D8           CLD
```